W9-BIX-035

Quartz
and Other Minerals

Chris and Helen Pellant

Gareth Stevens
Publishing

Please visit our Web site at: www.garethstevens.com
For a free color catalog describing Gareth Stevens Publishing's list
of high-quality books, call 1-800-542-2595 (USA) or 1-800-387-3178 (Canada).
Gareth Stevens Publishing's fax: 1-877-542-2596

Library of Congress Cataloging-in-Publication Data

Pellant, Chris.
    Quartz and other minerals / Chris and Helen Pellant.
      — North American ed.
      p. cm. — (Guide to rocks and minerals)
    Includes bibliographical references and index.
    ISBN-13: 978-0-8368-7908-7 (lib. bdg.)
    1. Mineralogy—Juvenile literature. I. Pellant, Helen. II. Title.
    QE365.2.P45   2007
    549—dc22   2006035962

This North American edition first published in 2007 by
Gareth Stevens Publishing
A Weekly Reader® Company
1 Reader's Digest Rd.
Pleasantville, NY 10570-7000 USA

This U.S. edition copyright © 2007 by Gareth Stevens, Inc.
Original edition copyright © 2005 by Miles Kelly Publishing.
First published in 2005 by Miles Kelly Publishing Ltd., Bardfield Centre
Great Bardfield, Essex, U.K., CM7 4SL

Gareth Stevens editorial direction: Mark J. Sachner
Gareth Stevens editor: Alan Wachtel
Gareth Stevens art direction: Tammy West
Gareth Stevens designer: Scott M. Krall
Gareth Stevens production: Jessica Yanke

Picture credits: All artwork courtesy of Miles Kelly Artwork Bank. Photographs from the Miles Kelly Archives: Castrol,
CMCD, CORBIS, Corel, DigitalSTOCK, digitalvision, Flat Earth, Hemera, ILN, John Foxx, PhotoAlto, PhotoDisc,
PhotoEssentials, PhotoPro, Stockbyte cover, p. 28, p. 29; All other photographs courtesy of Chris and Hellen Pellant.

Printed in the United States of America

2 3 4 5 6 7 8 9 10 10 09 08

COVER: A crystal of quartz.

Table of Contents

Words that appear in the glossary are printed in
boldface type the first time they appear in the text.

What Are Rocks and Minerals?

- Many types of rocks and minerals exist on Earth. People use them in many ways. Rocks and minerals are also beautiful to look at.

- Minerals are solid natural substances that are made of the same material all the way through. Rocks are made of minerals. They are solid, but rocks are not the same all the way through.

- One example of a mineral is quartz. If you look at a **crystal** of quartz, you'll see that it is made of the same stuff all the way through. No matter how big the piece of quartz is, it is made of the same type of material all the way through.

- Granite is a type of rock. If you look at a piece of granite, you can see that it is made of different types of minerals. Quartz, mica, and feldspar are among the minerals in granite. Limestone and marble are two other types of rock. Both contain the mineral calcite.

- Scientists who study rocks and minerals are called **geologists**.

- Geologists place different types of rocks into groups. These groups are based on how the rocks form. **Igneous rocks** form from **molten** material that cooled deep within Earth or from molten material that erupted onto Earth's surface out of volcanoes. **Sedimentary rocks** form out of layers of tiny particles. **Metamorphic rocks** form when Earth's forces heat or squeeze rocks so much that they change into a different type of rock.

Minerals form in a wide variety of shapes. Many minerals form in crystals with flat surfaces. Some minerals form in crystals with rounded shapes.

In addition to being parts of rocks, minerals form in long, narrow bands called mineral veins. A mineral vein may run through a big piece of rock.

The salt we put on our food and the gemstones out of which we make jewelry are all minerals.

ABOVE and BELOW: Minerals can have bright colors and fine crystal shapes. The yellowish mineral ettringite (*above*) forms in six-sided crystals. Dioptase (*below*) has a rich green color. Its crystals have a vitreous, or glassy, **luster.**

Mineral Hardness and Color

- Geologists need to do many tests to tell one mineral from another. One of the things they test is how hard a mineral is.

- The hardness of a mineral is measured by how easily it can be scratched. In the hardness test, a mineral is scratched with objects of increasing hardness, including fingernails, knives, and other minerals.

- In 1812, Friedrich Mohs, a German **mineralogist**, created the mineral hardness scale that is still used today. Mohs' scale has ten points. Each point is defined by a well-known mineral.

- At point 1 on the hardness scale, talc is the softest mineral. It can be scratched with a fingernail. Diamond is the hardest mineral on the scale, at point 10. This highly prized gemstone is so hard that it is also to used to cut metal, stone, and even other diamonds.

BELOW: The ten points on Mohs' hardness scale are represented by well-known minerals.

1	2	3	4	5
Talc	Gypsum	Calcite	Fluorite	Apatite

- Color also helps geologists tell minerals apart. The color of a mineral depends on the **elements** that are in it.

- Minerals that contain iron, such as hematite and magnetite, are often reddish brown or black. Many minerals that contain copper, such as malachite and conichalite, are green. The minerals cinnabar and realgar contain mercury and are red.

- For thousands of years, people have used colored minerals to make paints and dyes. Malachite, for example, was used to make green paint more than 2,000 years ago in Egypt.

6	7	8	9	10
Orthoclase	Quartz	Topaz	Corundum	Diamond

Crystals and Mineral Shapes

- Minerals form in crystals. Most mineral crystals have flat surfaces. These crystals are also symmetrical, meaning that the surfaces of the crystal have the same shape. Some crystals form in cubes. Other crystals form in octahedra, or shapes with eight sides of the same size.

- All rocks are made of crystals of different minerals. For example, granite contains crystals of the minerals feldspar, mica, and quartz. You can see the crystals in granite with the naked eye. Many rocks, however, have crystals so small you need a microscope to see them.

- Some crystals are **transparent**. This means that light can pass through them.

- Some types of mineral crystals break cleanly along their flat surfaces. Other types of mineral crystals have rough edges when they break.

- In addition to color and hardness, geologists tell different types of minerals apart by the shapes into which they grow. When geologists talk about a mineral's habit, they are talking about the shape into which it grows.

LEFT: The "sun" shape of this piece of marcasite is a common habit for this mineral.

These small, reddish vanadinite crystals have a six-sided habit.

- Minerals come in a huge variety of shapes, or habits. Geologists have names for different types of mineral habits.

- The mineral hematite has a rounded habit. It forms in masses that are shaped like kidneys.

- Malachite, a green mineral, often forms in a habit that looks like a bunch of grapes.

- Goethite, a mineral that contains iron, often forms in a habit that looks like icicles hanging from the roof of a cave.

- Crystals of the mineral mica are flat and flaky. Because they look like a tabletop, mica's habit is called tabular.

BELOW: These are not the branches of a fossil plant but patterns formed by the mineral pyrolusite.

Quartz

- Quartz is one of the most common minerals. It is found in many different places, and it is present in most rocks.

- Quartz is made of the elements silicon and oxygen.

- Quartz can be found in a great variety of colors. Some colored types of quartz are used in jewelry. Amethyst (purple quartz), rose quartz (pink quartz), smoky quartz (black and dark brown quartz), and citrine (orange quartz) are all cut and polished for jewelry.

- Colorless, transparent quartz is called rock crystal.

- Quartz is the hardest common mineral. It defines the seventh point on Mohs' hardness scale. Quartz is so hard it cannot be scratched with a knife blade.

- Quartz often forms in six-sided crystals that come to a point at the top.

- Chalcedony is a type of quartz that is made of microscopic crystals.

LEFT: Amethyst is the purple-colored semiprecious form of quartz.

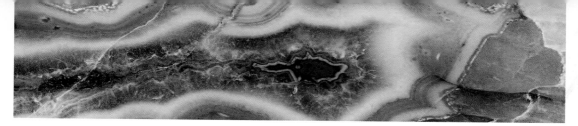

ABOVE: Agates have alternating colored bands. This agate has been cut and polished.

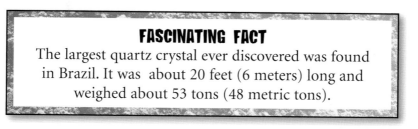

FASCINATING FACT

The largest quartz crystal ever discovered was found in Brazil. It was about 20 feet (6 meters) long and weighed about 53 tons (48 metric tons).

- Agate is a semiprecious stone that is made of the same elements as quartz. Agate forms in bands of different colors.

- In addition to being used in jewelry, small crystals of quartz are used in watches and electronic equipment.

RIGHT: This is a six-sided crystal of smoky quartz.

Feldspar and Mica

- Feldspar is the most common type of mineral in Earth's **crust**. It makes up nearly half of the basalt rock that covers the floor of the oceans.

- There are different types of feldspar. Most of them are pale in color, but some of them are reddish, bluish, or greenish.

- All types of feldspar contain the elements silicon and oxygen. The different types of feldspar contain various metallic elements in addition to silicon and oxygen.

BELOW: These blue-green crystals are a type of feldspar called amazonite.

- One type of feldspar is called orthoclase. Orthroclase contains the elements potassium and aluminum in addition to silicon and oxygen. This type of feldspar is common in the rock granite.

- Another type of feldspar is called plagioclase. Plagioclase is made with aluminum and either of the elements sodium or calcium. It is found mainly in basalt and rocks like it.

- People use feldspar to make pottery glazes, or coatings spread on pottery before it is baked in a kiln, and glass.

- Mica contains the elements potassium, aluminum, and iron.

- Mica is glittery and flaky. Because of the way it looks, mica is easy to identify.

- Mica is common in many igneous rocks, especially granite.

- One type of colorless or light brown mica is called muscovite.

- People use mica in making many things, including wallpaper and paints. It is also used in making the fake snow that people put on Christmas trees.

RIGHT: This glittery mass of mica has thin, flaky crystals.

Pyroxene and Hornblende

- The mineral pyroxene is formed in very hot **magma** and **lava**. Magma is molten rock within Earth out of which igneous rocks are made. Lava is molten rock that has come out of a volcano.

- Pyroxene can be nearly black, but it can also brown or dark green. Many **basic rocks** contain pyroxene. Pyroxene helps give basic rocks their dark color.

- Crystals of pyroxene are small and stubby.

- Pyroxene makes up about half of the rock gabbro. Gabbro is a type of igneous rock with a rough texture.

- The mineral hornblende looks a lot like pyroxene. Both are dark in color. But they belong to different groups of minerals.

- Hornblende has long crystals that look like threads.

- Hornblende forms in light-colored igneous rocks such as granite and porphyry.

RIGHT: Hornblende crystals are usually more slender than pyroxene crystals. You can see the long, threadlike crystals of this piece of hornblende.

- The metamorphic rock amphibolite contains a lot of hornblende.
- One way to tell pieces of pyroxene and hornblende apart is to break them. Pyroxene breaks into perfect corners, like the sides of a cube. Hornblende breaks into pointy corners, like the points of a diamond shape.

RIGHT: Pyroxene crystals are usually short and stubby. When they break, the pieces usually have flat surfaces.

Beryl and Tourmaline

- The minerals beryl and tourmaline occur in igneous rocks such as granite and pegmatite.
- Beryl is harder than quartz.
- It forms in fine, six-sided crystals.
- Beryl can be **translucent** or transparent, and it has a glassy luster.
- Beryl comes in different colors. Many of these different types of beryl are used as gemstones in jewelry. Green beryl is called emerald. Yellow beryl is called heliodor. Pink beryl is called morganite. Greenish-blue beryl is called aquamarine.
- Tourmaline is as hard as quartz.
- Some types of tourmaline are transparent.
- Tourmaline is used as a gemstone. It comes in more different colors than any other gemstone. Pink tourmaline is called rubellite. Green tourmaline is called elbaite. There are also blue, yellow, and gray-blue types of tourmaline.

BELOW: These crystals show some of the colors in which tourmaline is found.

ABOVE: This emerald formed in pegmatite rock. Emerald is green beryl.

- Some types of tourmaline crystals are green at one end and pink at the other.
- Black crystals of tourmaline that form in granite are called schorl.

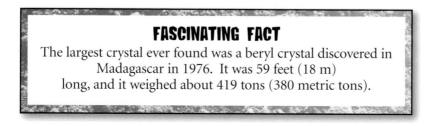

FASCINATING FACT

The largest crystal ever found was a beryl crystal discovered in Madagascar in 1976. It was 59 feet (18 m) long, and it weighed about 419 tons (380 metric tons).

Iron Ores

- Iron is an element that is a valuable **raw material**. One of its main uses is in making steel, a metal that is used to build many things, including skyscrapers and cars.

- An **ore** is a mineral that contains a valuable substance. Iron ores are minerals that contain iron.

- Most iron ore is found in sedimentary rocks. The biggest deposits of iron ore are in Canada, Australia, the United States, and Ukraine.

BELOW: This picture shows two different kinds of hematite: the reddish, rounded mass to the left and the black specularite around it.

- The mineral hematite is an iron ore that is either black or reddish in color.
- The reddish form of hematite has a rounded shape. The black form of hematite is found in tiny, black crystals. This form of hematite is called specularite.
- Magnetite is another mineral that is an iron ore.
- Magnetite is a hard mineral. It cannot be scratched with the blade of a knife.
- As its name suggests, magnetite is magnetic. This means that it pulls iron toward it. The mineral's magnetism is strong enough to move a compass needle or to attract tiny iron filings. People hiking in an area where the rocks contain magnetite cannot trust their compasses. The magnetite prevents the compass needles from pointing in the right direction.
- The island of Tenerife, which is located off of northwest Africa, has beaches made of black magnetite sand. This sand is made by the **weathering** of lava. Weathering is the process by which the forces of weather break rock into tiny pieces.

Diamond and Graphite

- The minerals diamond and graphite are two forms of the element carbon. They could not be more different in appearance.

- Diamond forms in small, glassy crystals. Often, diamond crystals have eight sides.

- Many diamonds are believed to be over 3 billion years old.

- Diamond is the hardest mineral. It defines the tenth point on Mohs' hardness scale (see pages 6–7).

- Diamonds are very valuable as gemstones. Because of their hardness, they are also used in factories for cutting.

- Graphite forms in flat, platelike, six-sided pieces. Theses pieces can have a dull, greasy, or metallic appearance.

- Graphite is very soft. It can easily be scratched with a fingernail.

ABOVE: This diamond has been cut in a way that shows off its sparkle.

BELOW: Diamonds occur in a rock called kimberlite. This kimberlite is from South Africa, and it has two small diamond crystals.

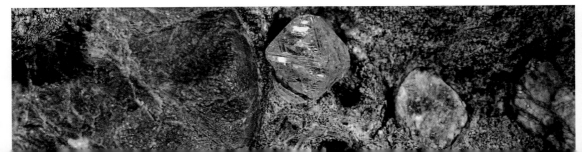

Native Elements

- Minerals made of a single element are called native elements.

- In addition to diamond and graphite, the group of native elements includes metals such as gold, silver, and copper, and nonmetals such as sulfur.

ABOVE: Sulphur's bright yellow crystals are clearly visible. This piece of sulfur is from Mexico. Sulphur has many uses in industry. Sulphuric **acid** is important in making chrome-plated metal.

- Native-element metals have many uses. Gold and silver are widely used in jewelry. Platinum is used in the catalytic converters found in many cars. Copper, which conducts electricity well, is used in wiring.

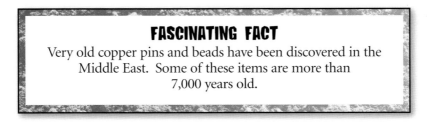

FASCINATING FACT
Very old copper pins and beads have been discovered in the Middle East. Some of these items are more than 7,000 years old.

Sapphire and Ruby

- Sapphire and ruby are both forms of the mineral corundum.

- Ruby is bright red corundum. Sapphire is blue corundum. Corundum can also be pink, yellow, gray, green, and brown.

- Corundum usually forms as six-sided crystals that have pyramids at the top and bottom.

- Corundum is the second-hardest mineral.

- Because it is so hard and so colorful, corundum is valued as a gemstone.

- Corundum forms in igneous rocks and metamorphic rocks. Most of the corundum used in jewelry is found in river shingle, or large gravel-like pieces found on the banks of rivers. Gem corundum is found in Sri Lanka, Kashmir, Australia, Thailand, and Africa.

- Some rubies and sapphires have needles of rutile, another mineral, in them. These gemstones look as if they have a star in them.

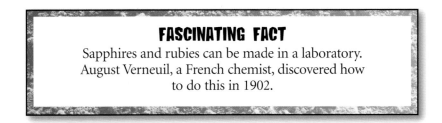

FASCINATING FACT

Sapphires and rubies can be made in a laboratory.
August Verneuil, a French chemist, discovered how
to do this in 1902.

ABOVE: These ruby crystals from India are in a type of metamorphic rock called gneiss. The light-colored crystals around the rubies are quartz.

Fool's Gold

- The minerals pyrite and chalcopyrite look like gold. Because these minerals are often confused with gold, they are called "fool's gold."

- Pyrite has a silvery yellow color that does not look that much like real gold but can fool people from a distance. Chalcopyrite has a deep yellow color that is closer to the color of real gold.

- With a few simple tests, it is easy to tell fool's gold from the real thing.

- Real gold is so soft that you can scratch it with a coin or dent it by biting down on it. Pyrite, however, is so hard that it cannot be scratched with a knife blade. If you bite pyrite, you will probably damage your teeth.

- Real gold does not change color when exposed to air. When chalcopyrite is exposed to air, it turns a variety of "peacock" colors.

- Both types of fool's gold are not as heavy as real gold. Compare a piece of fool's gold to a piece of real gold of the same size, and the real gold will always be much heavier.

RIGHT: Pyrite forms as cube-shaped crystals with lines on the faces of the crystals.

- Pyrite is a common mineral. It is found in mineral veins, metamorphic rocks, sedimentary rock, and some igneous rocks.

- Chalcopyrite is valuable as an ore of copper, which is used to make wires that conduct electricity.

RIGHT: Chalcopyrite has a richer yellow color than pyrite. It is also softer than pyrite. Chalcopyrite can be scratched with a knife blade.

Strange Mineral Properties

- Certain minerals have unusual properties. In many cases, they can be identified by these properties.

- The mineral Iceland spar is a transparent crystal of calcite. When people look through a piece of Iceland spar, they see double.

- Many minerals react with acids. When the mineral galena comes in contact with hydrochloric acid, a gas called hydrogen sulfide is released. This gas smells like rotten eggs.

- Certain minerals that contain iron are magnetic. Magnetite attracts iron. Hematite becomes magnetic when it is heated.

- Crystals of minerals such as ruby and sapphire can have a star-shape inside them. The star is thin pieces of rutile, another mineral, within the crystal.

- Quartz, tourmaline, and hemimorphite become charged with electricity when they are struck.

- Mica is brittle, but it can be bent — if you are very careful not to break it.

RIGHT: This piece of magnetite has attracted a paper clip.

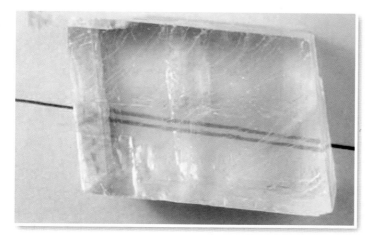

LEFT: When looking at a line through a piece of Iceland spar, you will see two lines.

- When a very hot flame is held to a mineral, the color of the flame changes. The new color depends on the elements in the mineral. Minerals containing sodium turn the flame yellow; minerals containing copper turn the flame green; and minerals containing potassium turn the flame violet.

- Many minerals are poisonous. Orpiment and realgar are two brightly colored minerals that are used in making paint. Both of them contain the element arsenic, which is poisonous.

RIGHT: Realgar, which is poisonous, has a rich red color and a greasy look.

Minerals at Home

- If you look around your home, chances are you will find plenty of minerals. Minerals are used in making all kinds of everyday things. Some minerals are even used in food.

- Cement, which is used to hold brick and stone together, is often made with the mineral calcite.

- Concrete is a common building material that includes cement and sand. Sand is made mostly of tiny pieces of the mineral quartz.

ABOVE: Today, one of the main uses of lead is for the plates in car batteries. Lead is obtained from galena.

- Many walls inside houses are covered with plaster. Plaster is made mostly of the mineral gypsum.

- Electricity is carried through a house in copper wires, and water flows through copper pipes.

- Anything made of steel could not have been made without minerals. Steel support beams, furniture, and cutlery all depend on iron ores — minerals such as hematite and magnetite.

- Talcum powder is made from the mineral talc. It is found in many bathrooms.

- The glass used in windows and drinking glasses is made from quartz sand. Quartz sand is melted and shaped into sheets or shaped into **vessels**. About 2,000 years ago, the Romans were the first people to make glass.

- The salt that people put on many foods is the mineral halite.

- The mineral galena is used in car batteries.

FASCINATING FACT
Accurate clocks and watches use very thin slices of quartz crystals to keep time. Even the clocks inside computers use quartz crystals.

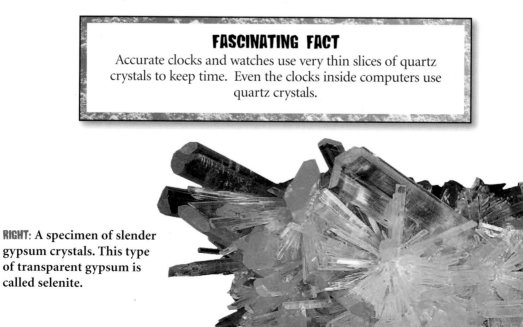

RIGHT: A specimen of slender gypsum crystals. This type of transparent gypsum is called selenite.

Glossary

acid: a chemical that has a sour taste

basic rocks: dark-colored igneous rocks that are made of feldspar, olivine, pyroxene, and a small amount of quartz

crust: a hard outer layer or covering

crystal: a piece of a transparent mineral that can have a shape with a regular arrangement of flat surfaces and angles or a rounded shape

elements: the simplest natural substance

geologists: scientists who study the layers of Earth and the rocks and minerals that make up Earth's crust

igneous rocks: rocks that have formed from the cooling and hardening of magma

lava: molten rock that flows from a volcano or the rock that forms when this substance cools

luster: the shine or reflection of light off an object's surface

magma: molten rock inside Earth that becomes igneous rock when it cools

metamorphic rocks: rocks that have been formed by the forces of heat and pressure within Earth

mineralogist: a geologist who specializes in minerals

molten: melted

ore: a mineral from which a valuable substance can be removed

raw material: material that is worked, combined, or changed into new, useful products

sedimentary rocks: rocks that have formed from the small pieces of matter deposited by water, wind, or glaciers

translucent: letting some but not all light through

transparent: letting light through so that objects on the other side can be seen clearly

vessels: containers such as bottles, cups, or bowls used for holding something

weathering: the effect of wind, rain, and changes in temperature on a material that is exposed them

For More Information

Books

Experiments with Rocks and Minerals. True Books: Science Experiments (series). Salvatore Tocci (Children's Press)

Minerals: From Apatite to Zinc. Exploring Science (series). Darlene R. Stille (Compass Point Books)

Rocks and Minerals. Science Files (series). Steve Parker (Gareth Stevens)

Rocks and Minerals. Discovery Channel School Science (series). Anna Prokos (Gareth Stevens)

Salt. Rocks, Minerals, and Resources (series). John Paul Zronik (Crabtree)

Web Sites

The Dynamic Earth: Gems and Minerals
www.mnh.si.edu/earth/text/2_0_0.html
From the Smithsonian Institution, this Web site features multimedia presentations on gems and minerals

The Dynamic Earth: Rocks and Mining
www.mnh.si.edu/earth/text/3_0_0.html
Also from the Smithsonian Institution; check out "Minerals Matter"

Mineral Matters
www.sdnhm.org/kids/minerals/index.html
From the San Diego Natural History Museum, this Web site contains information on mineral identification and collecting, as well as games and how to grow crystals at home

Index